About the A

Melissa Davies is a writer and poet c ... She began writing poetry at school and had h ... poem published in an anthology when she was 14 years old. The anthology was a Christian publication which was supposed to show people's relationship with God but Melissa's poem was about a boy she fancied at school (and she isn't even slightly religious. Being a teenager is a confusing time).

Since then, luckily, she has become much better at submitting things that are relevant and her work has appeared in publications across the UK, Australia and the US.

After living in Perth, Western Australia for eleven years Melissa has now returned to the UK, where she lives in a tiny flat by the beach where she spends most of her time watching seagulls battle against the wind.

Twitter: @melissajdavies_

Facebook: @daviesmelissaj

www.melissajdavies.com

PINEAPPLES IN THE POOL

PINEAPPLES IN THE POOL

MELISSA J DAVIES

Unbound Digital

This edition first published in 2018

Unbound

6th Floor Mutual House, 70 Conduit Street, London W1S 2GF

www.unbound.com

ISBN (eBook): 978-1-912618-63-7

ISBN (Paperback): 978-1-912618-62-0

Design by Mecob

Printed and bound in Great Britain by Clays Ltd, Elcograf S.p.A.

For Dad, who taught me to always look for four-leafed clovers
And Mum, who showed me how to be strong.

Dear Reader,

The book you are holding came about in a rather different way to most others. It was funded directly by readers through a new website: Unbound.

Unbound is the creation of three writers. We started the company because we believed there had to be a better deal for both writers and readers. On the Unbound website, authors share the ideas for the books they want to write directly with readers. If enough of you support the book by pledging for it in advance, we produce a beautifully bound special subscribers' edition and distribute a regular edition and e-book wherever books are sold, in shops and online.

This new way of publishing is actually a very old idea (Samuel Johnson funded his dictionary this way). We're just using the internet to build each writer a network of patrons. Here, at the back of this book, you'll find the names of all the people who made it happen.

Publishing in this way means readers are no longer just passive consumers of the books they buy, and authors are free to write the books they really want. They get a much fairer return too – half the profits their books generate, rather than a tiny percentage of the cover price.

If you're not yet a subscriber, we hope that you'll want to join our publishing revolution and have your name listed in one of our books in the future. To get you started, here is a £5 discount on your first pledge. Just visit unbound.com, make your pledge and type DEV18 in the promo code box when you check out.

Thank you for your support,

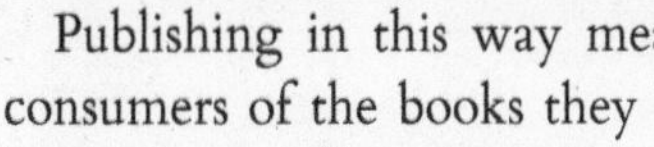

Dan, Justin and John
Founders, Unbound

With grateful thanks to Toby Wyles who helped to make this book happen.

Super Patrons

Stax & Bones
Shona Adams
Sheryl Andrews
A B
Jennifer Baker
Alicia Bakewell
Jennifer Bannon
Rowena Beaton
Anita Bishop
Hannah Born
Fleur Bragaglia
Kate Bulpitt
John Butler
Andrei Cabasa
Yvonne Carter
Laura Chidgzey
Wesley Coverdale
Desiree Crossing
Alexandra Curthoys
Ben Davies
Liselotte Davies
Amy Dawson
Amy Doherty
Debbie Ducic
Char Edmonds
Jacqui Edwards
Cassandra Edwards
Fayth Eloise Good
Shaun Ensom
Katy Evans
David Foster
Mary Gill

Jessica Graham
Lizzie Grosvenor
Cris Hale
Chloe Harris
Esther Harris
Lauren Hepple
Thom Hill
Paul Holbrook
Ella Homes
Sabrina Houssami-Richardson
Steve Hughes
Belinda Johns
Michelle Johnston
Brenda Jones
Sarah Jordan
Jenna Keogh
Dan Kieran
Floss Lemmon
Russell Lockyer
Frances Lodge
Charlie Loft
Eva Lomski
Emma Longhurst-Gent
Heather Lowe
Emma Luffingham
Jamie Macdonald
Daniel Madden
Jessica Marshall
Celine Marston
Katy McGhie
Anna McLeish
Sally Mead
Cameron Michael
Bob Miles
John Mitchinson
Melissa Moore

Brian Morris
Sarah-Jane Mullane
Debra Murphy
Carlo Navato
Jerry Nolan
Ryan Norrish
Mae North
Lauren O'Brien
Chantelle O'Connor
Lev Parikian
Emily Paull
Michael Petrovski
Lauren Pilbeam
Jack Pinnington
Justin Pollard
Jason Price
Jaclyn Rankin
Eric Reid
Steven Robertson
Frances Robinson
Christina Rose
Laura Rowley
Erin Scales
Ami Sibbick
Michael Smith
Amelia Smith
Alex Tate
Sam Taylor
Jo Thornton
Phil Tickner
Jan Tickner
Sophie Ward
Angie Ward
Lauren Waye
Claire White
Julie Wilson

Katy Wimbush
Georgina Wood
Gina Wyles
Toby Wyles
Debbie Yates

Contents

My geriatric vagina

I'm thirty-four and a third
and I am told
that if I want to have a child
I have to do so soon because
after thirty five
pregnancy is not a normal pregnancy
but a geriatric pregnancy
I expect that in eight months
my vagina will shrivel
and become an old lady
separated from the rest of my body
by a slice of grey
it will start to knit
and bake scones
it will call younger people
"dearie"
and offer unsolicited life advice
while shouting at cheese.
My vagina will need its own
distress button
in case it has a fall
or it will be moved into a
care facility and forgotten about
because who cares about old people
let alone my geriatric vagina?

Various states of

Undress me outside the casino
while I lower my expectations.

Lay me bare in the park after dark
while I mistake greed for hunger.

Strip me down by the chicken shop
while I validate your masculinity.

Disrobe me behind the supermarket
while I confuse attention for love.

Expose me by the off licence
just don't call me *babe.*

Serpentine Lane

September when I first noticed her.
Sneaking into the garages opposite my flat.
The block had been sold and
the garages were empty, in disrepair. Steel
roll doors hanging off and holes in the roof.
Just before dark, checking around her
before she opened the wooden door that
no one had bothered to lock. I saw her a
few days later, nestled in a sleeping bag
on the High Street.
Eyes pale.

More people arrived. Louder now.
Men joking around and pissing up the wall.
They shouted to each other and let
the gate slam. They banged on the other
garage doors in the mornings to wake up
their mates. They didn't wait till dark like
her to come and go.

She disappeared.

Then…
On a day when the wind screamed
down the lane so cold it stole your breath
away, a padlock appeared, a thick heavy
chain through the gate. Mattresses and
bedding discarded along the road.

Work men came, fluorescent jackets
glowed by streetlights. They pulled off

the doors, pulled down the roof. Collected metal and timber in the middle of the yard. Clearing the way for demolition. Development. Fancy flats for the middle classes where there's no room to be poor.

I still look for the girl now. I want to tell her that I'm sad too. I keep change in my pocket in case hers is one of the faces I walk past. I want to tell her that I want to help her but don't know how. I want to tell her that I see her and that no matter how deep, no one can shelter within their own wounds.

A short poem dedicated to Dev Patel

I tried to write a poem
full of meaning and
important things,
about the way the world
feels to me,
the sorrow and the lies.

Instead I find myself
staring into space,
thinking of the gentle kindness
alive in Dev's handsome eyes.

Things that men have said I am

too clever
too dumb
too out of luck

too needy
too distant
too proud of myself

too messy
too boring
too quick to judge

too loud
too sharp
too fat to fuck

too frigid
too flighty
too hard to please

too fickle
too focused
too much of a slut

too boisterous
too lazy
too muddled up

I was woken once in the middle of the night

I was woken once in the middle of the night,
a nightmare,
so I messaged you.
I knew that where you were it wasn't late
and I pictured you in your flat listening to records
with a can of beer on the stool you used as a table.
You asked me what my nightmare was about
and I had to lie,
I told you that we had to run from room to room and
I made it sound ridiculous without meaning to
and then when you laughed it made me cry.
I can't tell you that I really dreamt of you
not belonging to me anymore,
of the day when we had finally said goodbye,
when I can't then text you in the middle of the night
without you asking, *why*?

A Love Letter to Nurses

(for Mel Stormy Moore)

My friend Mel plays roller derby.
We started at the same time and she got
much better much quicker than I did.
We used to sit on my porch and drink beer until day light and once she was sick in my kitchen and my housemate had to clear it up because
I had already gone to bed.

My friend Mel is a nurse.
She tells me stories about things
found up people's bottoms and disgusting
fluid that comes out of people.
I imagine her sitting in a nurses' room
with a plastic crate full of lightbulbs and action figures.

She never tells me about the other things,
the caring and the kindness,
holding hands with a patient who's scared
or the reassuring words gifted to a relative.

No. We talk about skating or vomit, broken bones or busted ribs.
I've never asked her how nurses hide
superhero capes beneath their scrubs.

Shouting

My neighbour is shouting.
about something I cannot see.
Sometimes he sings.
Sometimes he laughs.
But mostly he shouts,
shouts at his wife about nothing at all.
My neighbour is shouting.
I think he needs to get in the sea.

The 19th anniversary of my friend losing her virginity in a field by my parents' house

we're sitting around a table heavy with roast dinners. the first time the four of us have been together in years. marriages have happened. babies. break ups and heartbreak and all of the things in between.
I say, 'This birthday I will be closer to fifty than to twenty'.
Silence for a second, then,
'oh fuck.'
Then,
'your next birthday will be the nineteenth anniversary of me losing my virginity in a field by your old house…'
Silence, then,
'Oh, fuck.'
We're laughing until we're holding our bellies and our faces hurt and we're all talking at once, like,
'Oh shit, yeah, was that…'
and
'Argh, I remember! He was…'
'Preeetty hot'
'Have a vagina party to celebrate!'
'I mean, not *awful*…'
My friend picks up a piece of ham her daughter dropped on the table and my other friend's baby starts to hiccup and both of them go back to being mums for a second before someone says, 'Do you remember when…' and we're howling again and other people in the pub turn to look at us but we're fifteen and stealing nail varnish from Superdrug and smoking stolen cigarettes so we don't see their disapproval.
As we leave we hug those big full body hugs that come from a lifetime of knowing,
of lost virginities in fields,
of bunking off from school and all those things done together and all those things done apart,

of being closer to fifty than twenty and having those hugs that come from a lifetime of knowing.

You remind me of everything I have ever been interested in

Reading poems in a hammock and drinking tea made from loose leaves.

Roaring fires and that feeling in my belly from too much mulled wine.

Playing hopscotch in the rain and eating crisps in my underwear.

Staying up late for no reason other than watching one more episode.

Leather notebooks with warm thick paper and dusty purple ink for fountain pens.

Warm summer days drinking pear cider from a condensation covered glass.

How a bright sun and low fog can turn the world to a sepia-stained watercolour.

A haiku for Dev Patel

Dev Patel, oi!
I think you're pretty fit.
Marry me. Please.

I'm sorry for the things I said when I was drunk

~~I don't know why it happens, but sometimes I drink too much wine and I decide that I have to fix things. It's like suddenly I have all the answers and I know what to say to make everything right again. I don't. I'm sorry for the things I said when I was drunk. When I was over eager and intense, when I forgot that you don't share my brain and aren't thinking about the same things I'm thinking about.~~

Itchy

I have written more poems about Dev Patel than about you but I think I like you more because sometimes when I look at you I get that feeling in the back of my throat like I'm about to get a cold but then I don't.

Exposed

I send a picture
of myself
lying on a rug
of oriental red and teal.

My eyes hint
at a flirtatiousness
I do not feel.

As soon as I see
delivery confirmation
I regret it.

I hope you can't tell
how exposed I am,
nothing
to do with
how little I'm wearing.

Discussing the benefits of chia seeds in a Swiss supermarket

'Here, let's get these,' Mum says, pulling a box of chia seeds off the shelf. I pull a face. 'What,' she says, as she puts them in the trolley. 'I just don't think they're very good for you, Mum. They don't have much nutritional value. They're just bollocks.' She raises an eyebrow. 'You used to swear by them.' she says. I try to think back to a time when I would have sworn by chia seeds. I remember when I was all into paleo and got a bit thinner by basically eating three cows a day and exercising like I had mad cow disease. I hated myself and my body and everything that was happening in my life. I remember when I *was* that person who swore by chia seeds because "oh-my-god-they-are-just-so-good-for-you-like-just-the-best" when really I just thought they were good because all the paleo blogs told me they were and if I ate them I didn't feel like eating much else. I remember when I was a person who read a lot of paleo blogs and thought a lot about food and tried not to eat any. 'Well, get them if you want Mum, but just know that it'll look like there are tadpoles swimming in your poo.'

Rotting comfort

We lie together,
him and me,
in a bed made from
rotting comfort.

The pillows
are bundles of
twigs and leaves
dragging my hair.

For a quilt,
piles of moss
knitted together
with desperate pleasure,

with desperate pleasure
knitted together
piles of moss
for a quilt.

Dragging my hair,
twigs and leaves
are bundles of
pillows.

In rotting comfort
our bed is made,
we lie together,
him and me.

Just give us a day

where the sun rises across
a perfectly ordinary sky,

where a woman can walk
home alone
and children can play on
the street,

where girls can safely
go to school
and no one religion is blamed
for every evil,

just give us a day
where we don't have to
stare at a screen and ask
what's next or wonder *why*.

Just give us one day.

Life according to Dizzee Rascal

If Dizzee Rascal was a greengrocer instead of an internationally acclaimed pioneer of grime, would he know the fibre content of mangos and not recommend people eat them for breakfast?

Would he sing songs to himself about how big corporations and supermarkets treat small business owners and rob High Streets of their heart instead of songs about waking up in a daydream and baselines and silence?

Would he say, "How'd ya like them apples?" to people enquiring about the origin of a Granny Smith, would he recommend for a tart the sharpness over the crispness of a Red Delicious?

My heart breaks a little each time

a man with a gun,
a knife,
a car,
decides his cause or belief
is more important than
the lives of others.
I scroll past the images of destruction,
past the blame and anger,
past the pointing fingers and the hate,
I scroll until I can find the kindness,
the help,
the hope,
anything that stops once-solid ground
from shaking beneath my feet.

Curled confetti

I still sleep on the mattress we shared.
Your side is occupied by a cynical ghost
mine sags from the weight of my body.
There is a cardboard box on the floor
smelling of cigarette smoke and anger.
Wisps of sadness. The cat has scratched
the box so that it is surrounded
by a moat
of beige and curled confetti.
I leave it there to remind me
that power comes from freedom
and this freedom is priceless.

Guarded

shouting, scowling,
pen in hand,

the roar of the train,

he stands,
his head hanging,
pen scratching notepad,

I think:

how can you
expect him to
pay a fine

when he's carrying his bed in his hands?

Pineapples in the pool

Loving you is like
sitting on a trampoline while someone else does flips and waiting to see if the next jump will be the one to throw you off the edge,

it's like
sleeping with the fan on all night because you like the way the air brushes your skin but you wake up in the morning with a dry throat,

it's like
being provided with a work lunch right before a big presentation and being too nervous to eat,

it's like
finding a perfect dress but the only one in your size has a hole where the fabric meets the zip and you're not handy enough with a sewing machine to fix it,

it's like
writing my first name and your surname but scrunching it up and throwing it in the bin so no one can see it,

it's like
throwing pineapples in the pool and not knowing if they're going to sink or float.

A second short poem dedicated to Dev Patel

Don't tell me you haven't
ever thought about how
very handsome he is,
peering out
at you from the
telly, in Lion, or even the Best
Exotic Marigold Hotel (the greatest film ever made)
like the duckling who grew into that swan.

Inadequate vocabulary for grief

Time heals all. One day this wound will be blurred at the edges like an old photograph. The edges warn and frayed. The paper yellowed.

Everything happens for a reason. The world will keep on spinning and even though it should spin off its axis and hurtle into space it won't.

Life goes on. Your life will continue as it always has. You will become so accustomed to this emptiness that one day you will stop pulling at it with your fingers.

You have to keep busy. Organise your face into a portrait of sadness but not so sad that it makes people uncomfortable. Repeat this over and over until you are Picasso.

Silver

I know it feels as though
the moon has dropped
out of the sky,
and the ground you trusted
to stay
solid
has thrown you
into the dark

and what can only be
described as the chaos of
a burning wasps' nest

but it is impossible to believe that
you are not made of silver
and
stardust

and that one day
you will not find yourself again.

Stormbird

I hold in my hand a tiny
feathered ball of feeling,

skull so tiny and precious,
hollow bone,

I clasp my hands softly
protecting it from harm,

from all the things I
am scared of,

an uneasy safety

it flutters,
wings like straw against my palms,

my stormbird
aching to be free.

I went to see a psychic

once

when I was very sad

I had an ex who didn't like the combination of chicken and

cheese

I wonder if I would have had better luck teaching

abstinence

to my cat rather than trying to get reassurance

from

a

{quack}

What have I got to write about

Your world
so different to mine,
air conditioned offices,
comfortable chairs,
endless emails.

Yours is boiling point,
red dirt and cracked heels,
remote stations and
precious maleness.

You think mine is pampered.
I think yours is toxic.

What have I got to write about?

If not poems about
pigeon grey clouds, dappled,
the prickle of air
fizzing on skin
before a storm.

If not poems about
the way a tiny glance can
erase a hundred broken promises
of lovers' touches and
kisses stolen in crowded rooms
like stars
when the sun arises.

What have I got to write about
if not poems about how
none of this
means anything to you.

I tried to take a picture

of a parrot that had flown onto a branch above me
I wanted to send it to you
so you could see what I see
how colourful, how rich the red
and bright and clear on a perfect autumn day.

But when I looked at the photo
with the light behind the bird
she was reduced to a dull grey
and I knew then that all you would see was this pigeon
where a parrot should be.

Sing a song of binary

0101001101101001011011100110011100100000011000010010000
0011100110110111101101110011001110010000001101111011001
1000100000011000100110100101101110011000010111001001110
0100001101000010100101000001100101011100100110100001100
0010111000001110011001000000111010001101000011001010010
0000011101000110100001101111011101010110011101101000011
1010000100111011100110010000001100010011001010110010101
1011100010000001110011011011110111011101100101011001000
0001101000010100101010001101111001000000111001101101001
0110111001100111001000000110000100100000011100110110111
1011011100110011100100000011011110110011000100000011000
1001101001011011100110000101110010011110010000110100001
0100101011101101000011010010110110001100101001000000110
0111011010010111001001101100011100110010000001100001011
0110001101100001000000110110001100101011000010111001001
1011100010000001110100011011110010000001100011011011110
110010001100101000011010000101 0

Sing a song of binary,
perhaps the thought's been sowed
to sing a song of binary
while girls all learn to code.

Songs on my playlist that no longer remind me of you

(search "Pineapples in the Pool" on Spotify*)*

I listen to the same twelve songs every
day
and now only seven of them remind me
of
you so I have to skip them as soon as I
hear
the first chords. I think that I would be
really
good at that game on quiz shows where
you
have to guess the song from the first bar –
but
only if those songs were the ones I always
skip.

A thin strand

A thin strand
holds us together,
a fibre so slight it can't be seen,
barely felt.
Like a spider's silk
it wraps around us,
weaving between us,
strung between lungs,
holding us in place.
Until it snaps
and we begin to spiral.

Adventures with Alzheimer's

Your hands are soft paper in mine
You have a full beard now, for the first time in your life.
It is white streaked with grey
I think it makes you look handsome, so I tell you and say that
I'm glad you are still trying new things
you laugh and say words that do not belong in a sentence together
you see mum and call out 'wife' which makes me laugh
because I'm glad you can still put a name to her, even though
it's not a name but what she is to you.

*

I wander from room to room while you sleep in the chair,
murmuring.
The tiles in the new conservatory feel warm
under my socked feet
I listen to the frogs in the pond that sound like ducks.
I decide that with your beard you look like an explorer
except now all you explore are your pockets
for hidden-away ice cream sticks.

*

We watch hours of Miss Marple and the Antiques Roadshow,
interspersed with ads for menopause treatment and exercise
equipment. You sleep again, legs crossed, head heavy on your hand.
I Google names of explorers to find one that looks like you. None do.
Later I will remember how thrilled you looked when I first arrived
and it will catch in my chest like something solid.

*

On the bookshelf in the room that was yours when you could
still negotiate stairs there is a book, sitting between

gardening manuals and paperbacks with cracked spines. It is
Fifty Places to Fly Before you Die. Cheerful title. I wonder why
dying is still the thing that we think of as the last hurdle
as if everything up to that point is fair game and you can do everything
like an octogenarian superman. Only later I realise the book is about fishing.

*

I bring you a glass of water and almost as soon as I put it down
you have tidied away crisps into it. I wash the glass out and refill it.
You do the same thing as soon as it's on the table and my back is turned and
I can feel my temper releasing from where it was tucked away below my ribcage and
as I am about to shout at you to not do it again, you wink.

Our March, 21 01 17

We come together
and stand
shoulder to shoulder,
side by side,
we use our words
to give voices to those
they try to silence,
we stand proud and strong
knowing power comes
from peace
not division,
we march
so they can see
we will fight
for unity,
solidarity,
equality,
and we will stand
solidly together,
shoulder to shoulder,
until this darkness turns to light.

I can't stop thinking about

I can't stop thinking about
the way that building burned

so close to wealthy neighbours
who live safely in a different world,

the pictures of the flames
against the night sky,

the voices of fire fighters
wondering how they wouldn't die,

the story of the boys who stayed when
their parents couldn't make it down the stairs,

the way the building had been built
of that cheaper cladding and no-one cared.

I can't stop thinking about
how I hope we never forget.

We will try again

until the heaviness of uncertainty exhausts us

until the earth stops spinning and falls off shoulders of giants

until the music stops and there is no longer any sound

until the moon stops rising and monsters begin to walk amongst us

until we fade away, our bodies brick dust and our eyes are as empty as our souls

we will try again

Windowsill

I lived once in a tiny flat at the top of a hill. It had a big window in the living room with a sill big enough to sit on. I put pictures on it. Pictures of my family and a boomerang my friends had signed when I left Australia.

The window in the bathroom didn't open and the fan didn't work so in the winter the damp lingered, getting into my lungs and turning all my beautiful dresses grey with mould.

The electric went off one night and when I called the landlord he told me about the box by the front door, the plastic token I had to take to the shop to put money on.

I had five pounds and that wasn't enough for food and electric so I ate plain rice I kept in the cupboard.

I spent a lot of time looking at the boomerang, thinking about the people who had left their mark on it.

This Place

for Aidan

This is the place
of blue skies and palm trees,
of beaches that stretch for miles
and where there is always time for wine.

This is the place
of warm evenings spent on
porches and in back yards, sinking
tins and spinning yarns until morning time.

This is the place
the land of the fair go.
Although this land isn't always fair
and not everyone will get a go.

This is the place
of salty oceans filled with
monsters in the depths, spiders
big as your hands, hiding behind blinds.

This is the place
of growing up and finding out
what it means to survive, and when I left
I left behind a part of this heart of mine.

On Grief

I carry my grief like a balloon tied to my wrist.

Sometimes it's full of stones and I have to scoop it up, hugging it close, heavy on my chest.

Sometimes the balloon is full of air. It trails along behind me so I almost forget it's there.

Sometimes the balloon is full of water. Thrown at me from behind, freezing me with shock.

Drenching.

The water will slowly dry but the balloon always reappears, tied to my wrist.

No. 8 Tram

The man puts his hand out to help me off the tram.

He is old. Perhaps mid-seventies. He has been to the ballet with his wife. I know because they have been talking about it, praising its beauty.

He makes me think of my father, a man who would always put his hand out to help a lady off a tram, to hold doors open, to help.

I think, perhaps, that I ought to be helping him. That I am more capable, more youthful, more able.

I thank him and grasp his hand as he offers it.

Smiling at Strangers

When the world around you is angry
and full of hate,
turn off the internet
and step out.

Maybe you'll see
a man you recognise, a poet,
having a yarn with some homeless blokes,
a woman walking three dalmations,
people practicing Tai chi in the park.

Buy some dinner,
something with cheese and potatoes
or a doughnut heavy with custard
perhaps a cake to share with work mates tomorrow,

and when you go home and wrap
yourself in a blanket to read,
after smiling at strangers,
the world around you might not seem
quite so bad.

"Enjoy today enthusiastically…

…for tomorrow soon will come
and we will be ashamed
of our vulnerability."

I wrote and sent that to Instagram.

You echoed it back to me
and I hated it,
proving my own point.

One day I'll be able to say

One day I'll be able to say
the words, 'I love you'
without feeling as though
I have had to let them go.

One day I will no longer
feel the pull of ghosts
through my words
tying me to something.

One day I will be able to say
the words, 'I love you'
without them sticking
like tar in my mouth.

The week of hospital

They speak in German so I don't really understand what they're saying. Until I do and then I wish I didn't. I try to ignore the "in his condition"s and "at his age"s. I think these phrases make him sound like a car. As if Dad's body is a vehicle that has seen better days. A vehicle that he should have sold long ago for a nearly new Renault Megané.

I have to concentrate to understand. I concentrate harder than anything I have concentrated on for months. Listening to the doctors talking to Mum in hushed tones, to Dad's groans, the nurses as they sooth him, watching how his arms jerk as though they have developed their own mind, totally separate from his normal stillness and quiet.

I listen so I can hear a slip up. So I don't miss something the doctors have said wrong. Done wrong. A misdiagnosis or an act of malpractice or a thread of something I can pull until everything unravels.

I listen for a reason to be angry.

And
I
am
so
angry.

Angry at the doctors for being so young. At the nurses for being so kind. At Dad for not upgrading to a nearly new Renault Megané. For being held hostage inside his own brain. At myself for being so impotent.

So unprepared.

So childish.
So unhelpful.

Whenever he can, we walk together.
Slowly.

We walk either side of him, Mum and I. Holding his hands and then beneath his arms when he gets tired.

I lend him the use of my legs because I am strong and he isn't. We walk the way we walked when I was a child, just graduated to walking from crawling. When he lent me his strength and before my own had been built.

I sit with my back to the hospital, sideways on the bench so I can lean my arm on the back and rest my head on my hand. I watch the bees float from flower to flower and listen to the people around me. Murmured conversations in a language I don't understand, the low drone of an air conditioning unit. It is peaceful noise. I feel peaceful with the sun on the side of my face.

It's the only time I sit in the sun now, when the nurses are with Dad, cleaning him, changing him. It's a relief. To hand him over and be myself again even though it's only for a few minutes.

To just be me and not have to lend anyone anything.

I stand in the shower at the end of the day, suspended between the need to be alone and the fear of loneliness tapping me on the shoulder. The grief that sits just above it, the smothering blanket that is so tempting.

I block my ears until the water sounds like rain, thick and heavy. The type of rain that takes weather reporters by surprise.

I stand there with my fingers blocking my ears until the sound turns hollow in my brain.

And I wonder if…

when the clouds become the earth
and the world turns in on itself,

when the sun becomes the moon
and that moon no longer shines,

when magpies are the eagles
and they have nowhere left to fly to,

when the mountains become craters
and lakes are brittle stone,

when asteroids fall away,
back to the deep space they were from,

when everything is reduced, I wonder if
you will still love me

when nothing
is the everything that it is.

Heaviness

'What do you talk about?', she asked, 'when you go and see your brain doctor?'

She blew on the steam coming from the mug in her hand. Tea made with the small hotel kettle and free bags. UHT milk that tasted like plastic.

'Just… things', he said. She frowned, waited for more.

The covers were crumpled around them, wrinkles in the stiff fabric like tiny mountains.

'How I'll never write a song as good as Teenage Kicks. How I don't have any clean socks. Heaviness.'

She had turned away and he could see the thin blue trails of veins, her skin white and thin.

'Heaviness', she repeated. 'Now that's something I can understand.'

She stood up and found her bra on the floor, snapping the straps into place.

For a while

after I am gone,
you'll continue to
find pieces of me
around your flat,
strands of my hair
on the pillow where
I slept, a hair band
under a
sofa cushion.
You won't notice
really, you'll just
pick them up, throw
them away. They might annoy
you, without your realising
why tiny reminders
get under your skin.
Then one day
there won't be
anything left. I wonder
if then you'll miss me,
and wish for something
to hold me close
to you
so you can remember
what it felt like
to have me breathing
beside you.

Scratch

I used to think that
we went together
like velcro

that our differences
would be what
held us
together

instead, you suffocate me with softness

and I scratch you with my teeth

When Adele gets sad does she listen to her own songs?

When she's rolling in the deep (cold shoulder),
when first love grows tired,
when hometown glory fades to a million years ago,
when sweetest devotion chases pavements,
when the one and only doesn't remember,
and a love song feels like a million years ago.

Does she set fire to the rain?
Accept that it's water under the bridge?
Turn into a daydreamer, wonder if she's saved the best for last, think it happened when we were young?

Does she say hello to love in the dark? Or send her love to your new lover? Does she have some remedy?

Or does she just allow her heart to melt to stone?

Mismatched

There are days where everything feels like it's in the right place, powerful and purposeful.

On those days I take selfies to send to someone I love in which I look like an over stimulated toddler.

There are days where everything is off, too bright, too loud, too much to take.

On those days I struggle to operate the automatic turnstile at the supermarket

The streets were full

of music and people and laughter and shouting.
The red wine seeped through her, his hand was warmth in hers.
She was running, laughing, drunk on happiness and he followed, holding on tight.
He stopped and pulled her back. Close to him. Her hands on his chest.
He kissed her nose. Then her lips.

Everything stopped.
For a second.

Then time sped up, the music, the lights, the sounds,
all happening too fast, too loud.
Another pub, the burst of heat walking in, the shouted orders over the noise.
Then running again. The anticipation of catching the train home.
He kissed her again, held her face and looked into her eyes to remember.
A gust of wind and brakes squealing on the tracks. The doors opening.

His hand pressed against the window, wordless.
The rain gathering on her coat as she watches him leave.

Salty Air

Whenever I have something to work through,
a trial or a sadness,
when someone close becomes a stranger,
I find myself at the beach.

I sit there until my face gets salty
and I think about
the colour of the ocean,
how the waves barrel
and dance together,
racing towards the shore.

If I'm lucky
whatever is stuck in my mind
becomes loose
and spills outwards
until it's whisked away by the wind.

Sometimes it stays
lodged

and I will sit a while
until my face gets salty and my hair
crisp,
until the sun dips and the wind
changes direction
and then I drive home
with sand between my toes.

Airport Hours

i. There is a woman in the sunglass shop wearing a headscarf in black and gold, a flowing kaftan of teal rainbows. She serves a customer, who walks out without buying anything, but her eyes remain gentle.

ii. People rush like ants carrying on their important business. snippets of conversation drift past like smoke from a candle.

iii. I sit on the floor opposite my gate and watch as people's feet amble by. I am chained to the wall by one per cent battery and the threat of a four-hour flight with nothing to read.

iv. I pass the time wondering who I would be friends with. The woman in red lipstick and Ramones T-shirt, tattooed arms. The old man reading a newspaper. Anyone with a smile in their eyes.

v. I can hear the concentration in his voice as he makes the announcement, trying to neutralise his accent.

vi. The man next to me introduces himself as Tony. He works on the ships. I don't ask which ships. I smile politely and put my headphones on, even though nothing is playing.

How can the sunshine make you happy when you long for the rain?

Is it the blood sport of finding someone magical?

The promise of getting away with it (all messed up)?

The loneliness of snakes and ladders and avoiding eating a panini on the toilet at 3am when you've sold your spirit to the disturbing trash mermaids?

Is it the fear of turning into a steampunk Ashley?

This isn't a Rachmaninoff competition (sorry, Mum),

it's liquid gas lighting surging through your veins then coming to a _____ with a mouthful of porn and tooth sensitivity,

you can't say everything in silence, sugar tits,

there's no *porque no los dos* for disappeared pleasure just because you don't know the difference between attention and love

and a perfect white-water love doesn't exist without eating ice cream quicker than you wanted to and even then your fist gets sticky.

Time to use that vapour, sweep all this under the carpet and dance with the devil in a pencil skirt.

The things I would show you if you could come to visit

I would make you sit on the window side of the number 950 bus so you can see all the buildings and people from the city all the way to my house. I would point out my favourite doorways and shop signs. I would tell you the story about how I once gave a woman a dollar because she seemed like she needed it more than me before I noticed she was carrying a David Jones bag. You would understand the reference to David Jones and would laugh at me, in that very kind way that you do.

I would show you my desk at work, not when anyone was actually in work of course, because we would both find that uncomfortable. You would like the plastic dinosaurs on my desk and you would tell me your favourite dinosaur fact. We would have a race across the empty office with wheelie chairs. I would win.

I would show you my house. We would sit on my porch and drink red wine until it got dark and the insects clambered towards the light like tiny hovercrafts. We would look at the stars and I would point out Orion and how he's upside down here, doing a somersault through the sky. We would spend hours lying on my bed with our feet on the pillows looking at the ceiling and talking about favourite records. You would tell me that your favourite thing about my room is the fireplace and how the light shines through my unwashed windows.

I would make you walk on the beach and I would pretend to really love the beach because in that moment, with you there, I would. We would walk with our feet in the water until they were itchy with sand and salt. You would try to pick up the water to throw at me and I would laugh at the silliness of that.

I would take you to my favourite pub and tell you stories of the things that happened there. The time my best friend started dancing even though the pub was empty and the bouncer laughed at her, how another time a friend fell backwards into a bush. And about how when I was very sad I would go there and listen to people talking about their lives and about how I'd write their stories down without them ever knowing.

I would show you all the rich parts of the city. The parts where the houses stood three stories tall and reached out towards the river. The parts that are all glass and polished concrete. Where office workers rush around full of their own importance. Then I'd show you the other parts, where the Deliveroo riders sit between shifts and the park where people wait for hours for the soup kitchen to open. You would understand that I want to show you the parts that are usually invisible, and you would understand why.

I would drive you to Kings Park where we would sit and look out over the city. We would walk among the trees and I would point out flowers to you and tell you things about them that I'd be *seventy* percent sure were true. You would think that I was very knowledgeable about Australian Native Flowers and I wouldn't say anything to put you straight.

We would go and eat at my favourite dumpling house on plastic chairs and formica tables. You wouldn't say anything about the slightly sticky surface or the cracks, instead you would eat the dumplings and talk about how delicious they were. You would use chopsticks and know to dunk them in vinegar but you would be a bit clumsy and we would laugh at your attempts to pick up a pork bun.

Take my hand and walk with me

to the darker end of town
past all the bars and well lit shops
past the buildings with their too-sharp edges
to where the men wear deep frowns
and the streets begin to narrow,
street art turns to tags
and pavers grow uneven,
shadows lurk in alleyways
and the lost remain hidden.

Take my hand and grow old with me
in the darker end of town.
We'll find a way to live these lives
in the way we know how
even when the night is long.

The best is yet to come.

Bonfire Night

(for Phil)

You stand with your arms round my waist
as pieces of firework float down,
making crowns of paper in our hair,
the air thick with burning, our eyes sting from it.

I can't see your face but I know
you're smiling just as widely as I am.

Acknowledgements

Thank you to Unbound: Kwaku Osei-Afrifa for commissioning *Pineapples in the Pool* to start with; James Peake for being my knight in shining grammar; Mark Ecob for the cover design and everyone else who has had a hand in making this book a reality.

To my early readers Emily Paull, Roll Darl, Basheera McKinnon and Matilda Oke, thank you for making me realise that this collection of not-stories could be made into something.

A thousand thank yous to the Pizza Slice Pals for all the wine and reassurance – Georgina Hannah Rose Cooper Wood, Ces, Grav, Wheels, Joffy Borker, Polly, Will, Minnie & Peets, Carney, and Aidan – my first pledger and constant shouty supporter. Thank you to Channy, who threw the first pineapple into the pool and provided me with such a great image to use throughout the pledging process. Thank you to Charlie for all the "pretentious creative type" chats while the book was still a fledgling.

Thank you to my family, I am so lucky to have been born into such a good one; special shout outs to Toby, who really excelled with godfather duties during the funding of this book, and Ben, who laid down the challenge of which sibling would be the first to be published. I'm happy to claim this as my win.

And finally, thank you to Phil, for holding my heart so gently and not minding that I wrote so many poems about Dev Patel.

Pineapples Float

Jesse Barker
Colleen Carney
Laura Chant
Jessica Coxall
Sonja Freeman
Pieter Jordaan
Rhiannon Kidner
Claire Lieb
Rebecca Liston
Minnie And PT LuckySkates
Matilda-Jane Oke
Tanya Stul
Wegmann Theres
Amanda Visbeen
Kellie Weston
Corn Wheelio

Pineapples Sink

Lisa Berry
Greg Brown
Simon Carville
Melissa Davies
Jack Howard
Chris Miles
Aidan Morgan
Kim Webb